HUGE

page 2

page 12

and Sara Vogler

Story illustrated by
Martin Aston

Heinemann

Find out about

- A huge ape-like creature called a Bigfoot

Tricky words

- huge
- ape
- metres
- hairy
- footprints
- filmed
- costume

Introduce these tricky words and help the reader when they come across them later!

Text starter

Some people say there are huge hairy creatures called Bigfoot living in some mountains in America. Many people do not believe there is such a thing as Bigfoot. They say that people have just made it up.

Bigfoot

People say they have seen
a Bigfoot.
They say it looks like a huge ape.
They say it is three metres tall
and it is very hairy.

Some people say if you see a Bigfoot it will run away. Some people say it will run after you.

Some people say it will kill you.

One man said he lived with a
Bigfoot family.
He said they were very tall and
very hairy.
He said they looked after him!

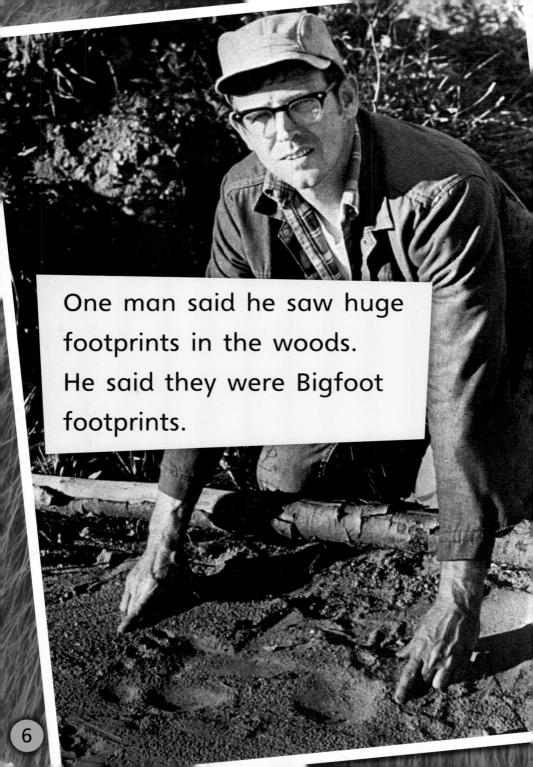

One man said he saw huge footprints in the woods. He said they were Bigfoot footprints.

But the man had made some huge feet and **he** made the huge footprints in the woods.

Two men went to look for
a Bigfoot.
They saw something in the woods.
They said it was a Bigfoot.

They said the Bigfoot was huge and hairy.

The men filmed the Bigfoot.

They said the Bigfoot saw them and ran away.

People saw the film.
Some people said it was a Bigfoot.
Some people said it was a man
in an ape costume.

What do you say?

Quiz

Text Detective

- Were the huge footprints made by a Bigfoot?
- Would you like to meet a Bigfoot?

Word Detective

- **Phonic Focus:** Initial consonant clusters

  Page 3: What are the phonemes (sounds) at the beginning of 'three'? Can you blend them?
- Page 4: Find the word 'some' three times.
- Page 7: Find a word made from two words.

Super Speller

Read these words:

away   huge   after

Now try to spell them!

HA! HA! HA!

Q What's white, furry and smells of peppermint?

A A polo bear.

In this story

 Jack

 Bigfoot

Tricky words

- climb
- mountain
- helicopter
- suddenly
- hairy
- roared
- hang glider

Introduce these tricky words and help the reader when they come across them later!

Story starter

Jack was just an ordinary boy, but he had a magic backpack. When Jack pulled the cord on his backpack – Pop! – something magic popped out. One day, Jack was reading about climbing mountains.

Jack and the Mountain

"I want to climb that mountain," said Jack. "I'll get my backpack."

POP! Out of his backpack came a helicopter.

Jack flew to the mountain.

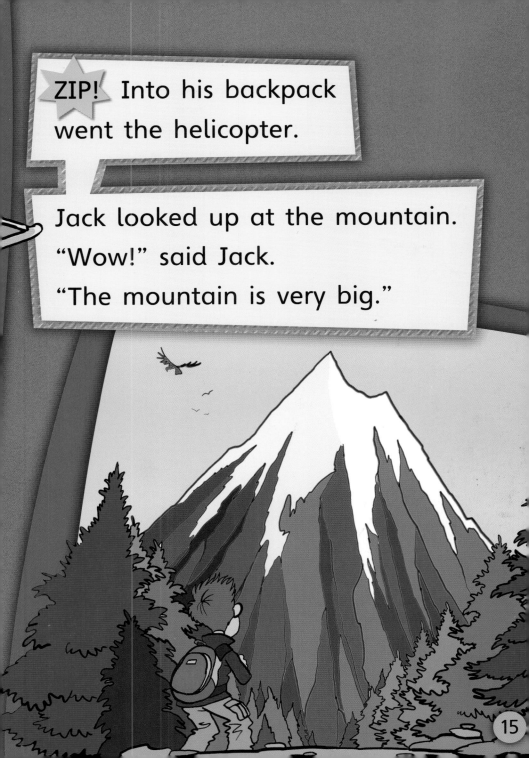

ZIP! Into his backpack went the helicopter.

Jack looked up at the mountain.
"Wow!" said Jack.
"The mountain is very big."

Jack started to climb
the mountain.
He climbed and climbed
and climbed.

Jack

Then Jack saw some footprints
– some very, very big footprints.

Suddenly, Jack saw something coming up the mountain.
It was very big. It was very hairy.
It saw Jack ... then it roared.

"Help!" said Jack. "It is a Bigfoot!"

Jack ran away.
He ran up the mountain.

The Bigfoot ran up the mountain after Jack. It roared and roared.

Jack ran fast.

The Bigfoot ran faster!

Will Jack get away?

Jack got to the top of the mountain.

"Aaargh!" said Jack. "The Bigfoot is coming!"

The Bigfoot was at the top of the mountain.

Jack grabbed his backpack. POP! Out of his backpack came a hang glider.

Jack flew off the mountain.

Quiz

Text Detective

- What was chasing Jack?
- Would you like a magic backpack?

Word Detective

- **Phonic Focus:** Initial consonant clusters
  Page 14: Find a word starting with two consonants.
- Page 13: Find a word with a silent letter at the end.
- Page 20: Find a word that means 'made a loud, angry sound'.

Super Speller

Read these words:

coming   fast   climb

Now try to spell them!

HA! HA! HA!

Q What's a Bigfoot's favourite game?

 A Swallow the leader.

EAR

COVENTRY LIBRARIES

Please return this book on or before
the last date stamped below.

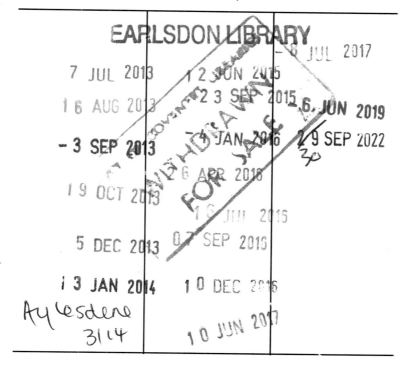
To renew this book take it to any of
the City Libraries before
the date due for return

Coventry City Council